Let Your Greatest Struggles Provide Your Greatest Opportunities

Erika Dawkins

Copyright © 2014 Erika Dawkins

All rights reserved.

ISBN: 0692363335
ISBN-13: 9780692363331

DEDICATION

I dedicate this book to my very special little boy. Without you I may not have found my place in this world.

CONTENTS

Acknowledgments
Confessions and Reflections
Introduction

1	Fear	11
2	The Reality Check	25
3	What They Say	35
4	Experience, Not Baggage	45
5	Prove Them Wrong	55
6	Be Your Best You	67

ACKNOWLEDGMENTS

I am extremely thankful for all of the people who saw me through this book.

To my parents and my sister, Shana, thank you for all of your support and understanding.

To my greatest friend, Ty, thank you for your faithful check-ins to ensure I stayed on track.

Vladimir, thank you for the constant encouragement and unwavering support you provided during this process, even when I made it difficult to do so.

A special thank you to LaShaia, for always providing a motivational word and reminder of what life is all about.

THE CONFESSIONS AND REFLECTIONS

The *Confessions and Reflections* is a book series that will allow you to get a closer look into the lives of individuals with very different experiences and backgrounds. Our hope is that you find books in the series that you can relate to and simply strike your interest and desire to learn more about the storyteller of the book.

Some of the books from this series will provide an opportunity for growth through reflection, while others will give you a front row seat in the lives of people who have had very interesting lifestyles. These stories will tell you how these individuals learned from their situations and how they became the person they are today.

You are about to read the first book from the series and it will provide plenty of opportunities for you to reflect on your own growth. Feel free to email us at info@erikadawkins.com to submit suggestions on the types of experiences you would like to read about.

ERIKA DAWKINS

INTRODUCTION

It was determined very early on in my pregnancy that I would be a single mother. In my mind, I knew this was not the way I had imagined things would be. At that time, my child was set to be born to a couple consumed by hostility, anger, and violence. The image of this spelled disaster.

At that point, I was still working out the details. Where do I go from here? How do I get out? These are things I had no answers to nor did I know who to consult that had experience with this. This was a very dark time. It was a time riddled with guilt and confusion as to where I would end up within the next few years.

I would like to say that today I have it all figured out. But the truth for most women is that we never totally have it all figured out—we just make it look like we do. My son is happy and healthy and seems to be experiencing a normal childhood—minus the presence of his birth father.

Who am I? Well, I guess it depends on whom you ask. I am a mother, a sister, a daughter, a business owner, a coworker, a writer, a friend, and now an author. Like many women I play many very different roles depending on the day and the situation. But my favorite role is and will always be Mommy. With all of that being said, I'm no one special, I'm just a regular girl with words stuck in my head that were destined to someday jump out and be read and hopefully related to by others.

Since the birth of my son I have had a craving to come across something to relate to, someone who was going through similar experiences with me, someone, anyone, that could give me the advice and encouragement I needed to help me recognize if I was actually going about life the right way.

I decided to write this book because I've read several books that were supposed to relate and provide advice to women and single moms. Several times I found myself experiencing a variety of emotions and asking myself several different questions:

> "Should I be resentful for my situation?"
>
> "How do I overcome my struggles?"
>
> "Should I be feeling lost and desperate?"

None of the books I read seemed to relate to my situation or my experiences as a woman over the years, and definitely didn't seem relatable to my experiences as a mom. Granted, I have only been in the mother role for a little over seven years. I have to consider that maybe I just haven't had time to reach the level of "womanhood" that those books are targeting.

Many of these books were more focused on how great things can become, not on the obstacles or how to prepare yourself for life. Very few of them provided the look inside that I needed. I wanted to hear personal experiences, horror stories, day-to-day emotions and feelings that women experience as they grow. I think I was looking for the realism in these books and I was unable to find that. I needed something more substantial that I could use to reflect and compare to what I was going through.

The most important part of this journey is learning how to make life work for you, and part of that is learning about yourself. Trust me, I get it—you already think you know yourself. But it took me some time to realize that Erika as a person and Erika as a mother are completely different women. Finding a middle ground is the hard, fun way to do it.

On my way to finding this middle ground I was left wondering whether I had the skills to successfully complete this journey of raising a young man who could be confident, successful, well rounded, and a positive contributor to the world, while also finding myself and accomplishing all the goals I set for myself. The moment I realized that I would be solely responsible for how these things develop was the moment I realized that this would all start in the way I think, conduct, and carry myself.

My goal in this book is to allow you into my world and introduce you to a process that has been beneficial for me while also giving you the opportunity to reflect on some of the things that many women and mothers experience at some point in their lives. Throughout this book I will share my experience and give some places for you to leave some reflections and experiences that you may have had. I like to confess and then reflect on the growth I've noticed within myself over the years, and this has given me the ability to look back and see my progress. Please feel free to use the spaces provided to think over some of your experiences and put your words down. The process of growth requires several stages. It took me quite some time to recognize those steps, but here is my method:

Step I: Confess

In the confession step, you recognize the areas or things you may need to grow from while also figuring out the things you need to let go of. By confessing these things, you are opening your eyes to the fact that these may be things that you don't need. Opening your mind to the fact that there are things in your life that aren't beneficial to you and recognizing them as a hindrance to you, on any level of life, shows the growth you are experiencing. After you embrace these things, write them down so you have something to reflect on later.

Step II: Reflection

Reflection gives you the opportunity to figure out why you no longer want to hold on to these things. It gives you the opportunity to put yourself back in that place. Sometimes actually putting things down on paper helps you to see them for what they really are. In reflection, you are able to go back and think of how those confessions that you want to let go of made you feel, how they affected you, and what you want to do differently.

Step III: Move

Once you have had the opportunity to confess and reflect, you have to find your escape. We go through this process to expose ourselves to the negative things in our lives. If you are anything like me and sometimes have a hard time letting go, then you may go through this process more than once for the same confession. That's okay—I always tell myself that repetition is the best way to learn.

By completing this simple process, I have learned to let go and work through many different things. You could say it's a form of therapy. I'm sure everyone around me would be happy to know that confessions and reflections have been the very reason that many of them haven't suffered life-threatening injuries. Just kidding. (Not kidding!)

We've all heard the relationship homework that requires a couple that is having trouble to write down the positives and negatives of the relationship, then weigh them up. If there are more positives then negatives, then work it out. The same goes for your life. Write these things down, reflect on them, and then move forward with how you choose to handle things.

I would like to provide you with the opportunity to confess and reflect on things that you may or may not be comfortable saying out loud, while also letting you know that it's okay to feel these things, as they are a part of what makes us who we are.

I provide my own confession and reflection after chapter one and you will have the opportunity to do your own at the end of every chapter. Each chapter ends with questions you should ask yourself and places to put your answers. Answering these questions should open your mind to a situation or situations that you can confess and reflect on.

I hope that within these pages you find something you can relate to while also learning that because your situation is less than or different than what you dreamed it would be, that you realize that it is all part of the process. From this, I hope that you are able to let go and relieve yourself of some of the stresses you may be holding on to and live a more abundant life through your experiences.

> *"Fear stifles our thinking and actions. It creates indecisiveness that results in stagnation. I have known talented people who procrastinate indefinitely rather than risk failure. Lost opportunities cause erosion of confidence, and the downward spiral begins."*
> - Charles Stanley

1 FEAR

The moment you realize your life, growth, and happiness are your very own responsibility (and nobody else's) is the moment you will begin to live a better life. This realization comes easier and more quickly for some and takes a bit more time for others.

I didn't always look at things that way. I was floating on cloud nine in a relationship I was sure would last a lifetime. It was one of those situations that you know is not perfect but that you are sure will change over time. The excitement of something fresh was there. I was able to visit a different city with new surroundings and more things to do. While these trips were often very exciting, they were at times quite interesting. I call them interesting because I was exposed to newer and more "adventurous" things than I had ever seen before.

I had a very normal upbringing. I grew up a military brat and with both parents at home. Many would say I lived somewhat of a sheltered childhood because of the fact that many of the things I learned about the world were learned through self-experience as they were not discussed at home—so, many of the things I was experiencing during this time were very new to me. While I knew these things were scary, I was so dumb and in love at this point that I didn't have enough sense to fear them. My focus was solely on living for that moment.

Nuptials were being planned after a six-month courtship, blindly and with a whole lot of excitement. I was trying on wedding dresses, looking at wedding venues, and expressing to everyone interested in hearing how excited I was to be getting married. I did all of this while remaining blind to the things that were glaring back at me. Like many women, I chose to turn a blind eye to the warning signs and instead focused on the future, where things could go and what it could be, certain that things would change for the better.

Throughout my visits, depending upon the day, there may be marijuana, cocaine, pills, and various other drugs scattered across the coffee table. Several of these, at that time in my life, I chose to consume as well. I surrounded myself with this for months. I enjoyed it for months. I was blind with my eyes wide open for months.

Drug use became a part of me; it brought clarity and a much-needed distraction from the things I wanted to avoid in life—a clarity I was not used to. The sensation of being able to escape all the painful parts of life and be numb from all the things I didn't want to feel was the most important thing to me.

This was a desire I absolutely kept from all of the important people in my life. A craving very few knew about. This desire was expressed to one friend, and her reaction is the reason it was never shared with any others. I was very good at disguising it; I functioned normally. I went to work, school, and home as if I had no cares in the world. The person I planned to spend my forever with introduced these things to me and I don't even think he realized the demon I struggled with.

I have always been an individual who walked to the beat of my own drum, so trying something new was not totally out of the ordinary for me, even as a child. The best way for me to learn and grasp something was through experience. I find it hard to simply take someone's word for something. I remember my parents telling me, "You just don't listen," "That would have never happened if you would have listened," or "You would be much better off if you would just listen." I wholeheartedly believe they felt this was true. But, it wasn't true for me. I needed to learn and experience things for myself and was always willing to accept the circumstances of the outcome, whether good or bad.

Not much changed as I entered adulthood. And while this was going on I cared nothing about how this would affect my future or my family. It was my experience and I was willing to bear the storm. All aspects of it. And I took that outlook into my relationship.

This relationship was a constant series of

emotions. Love, hate, anger, and hurt. A series of emotions that I don't think either of us truly recognized as a dangerous combination that was constantly full of arguing, cursing, violence, and threats. Then there were also days of joy and laughter. In hindsight, I think we were both afraid of each other for very different reasons.

One night, shortly after my arrival to his apartment, an argument began about a phone number written on a piece of paper on the floor in his apartment—that, of course in his mind, had to belong to me. At that point I was not interested in engaging in an argument and walked away to escape and relax in the bedroom. Simple confrontations such as this were not out of the ordinary, but through experience I learned that the best method for handling it was to walk away.

A few moments later the bedroom door flew open and then slammed shut. I stood in complete shock, with my back against the wall and his hands around my throat. It wasn't until this point that fear finally entered my body. Of course there had been confrontations before, but none that caused the level of fear I felt this time.

I had never been in that position before; I had never even seen it except for on television. All I could focus on was the tightness around my neck and the fear that this time I may not make it back to South Carolina, yet nothing in my body told me to attempt to fight back. I was frozen and could only stare directly in his eyes. The tightness was unbelievable and seemed to go on forever.

His grip eventually loosened as he spoke and I heard nothing but muffled sounds due to my focus on the ability to take in air again. And sadly, as scary as it was, this experience alone was not enough of an altercation to make me leave.

A few weeks following that night I learned I was pregnant, and it was then I realized that it was no longer about me. There was a baby coming into this; should he/she grow up seeing this? Are the drugs I've been using going to affect the development of my baby? There was no time to take these chances, and while I still hung in there a few months, I knew something very big would have to change. As his words the morning following that altercation played over and over in my head—"While you were asleep, I tried to think of a way to kill you and get your body out of here without the neighbors hearing"—I was reminded of the seriousness of this situation.

There were even times following this that I was convinced that I could stick it out. The arguing continued, but now with the emotions of pregnancy involved, leaving me a lot less tolerant of it. My non-tolerance only drove more anger into him. Who did I think I was to disregard him? He couldn't understand this, so I stopped visiting, I limited the conversations due to the content of them, and the words, "Well, if you are going to act like this then you need to have an abortion" were spoken. And from that I felt there was no need for any further conversation for us.

After this, I made the solid decision to leave the relationship behind and moved back in with my parents. I spent the next seven months working and going to school, only to be laid off a few months later. I continued with school and tried to keep myself sane, not knowing what was going to happen when my son arrived.

Most of my days consisted of confusion and crying, wondering what I was thinking putting myself in this situation and thinking of ways to escape it. Surprisingly, no one seemed to notice that while I appeared stable and seemed to be handling things successfully on the outside, I was slowly falling apart on the inside.

There were many days I felt defeated and there were days that I was willing to give up because it seemed much easier than having to listen to the thoughts that were in my head. I've had conversations with other women who said they had many of the same feelings I was experiencing. Some of these women were not single mothers, but simply women in general who were dealing with other things in life that were holding them back from the excitement that should surround them when embracing changes in their lives.

My goal was never to be a single mother, like many women, but the decision was made for me. Knowing that I would enter single motherhood from day one allowed fear to sink in even deeper. During this time I kept getting the feeling that it was too late to be scared. He would be here and I had to figure it out. That's the thing about fear—it overwhelms you and captures your thoughts.

My fear was not knowing what the future held for me, and also realizing that I would now have to deal with the outcomes of the decisions I made. Your fears may stem from something very different, however, our approach must be the same. We have to recognize those fears and uncover ways of overcoming them.

Confession:

I am the only person responsible for this experience. I allowed myself to participate and be a part of a very dangerous lifestyle. I put dangerous things into my body. I allowed myself to be destroyed emotionally and physically. These situations placed a fear in me that left me afraid of ever having to experience the feeling of a lack of control again. I stayed because I was afraid to be alone. The sound of a door slamming, someone putting their hands around my neck and having my back against the wall has the potential to take me back to that night. The fear of judgment has kept me from sharing this information with people. I have been very ashamed to share my experiences with abuse and drug usage. While I embrace all of the experiences as lessons, I still fear judgment from time to time.

Reflection:

I reflect and realize that each of these situations play a part in who I am to become as a person. Had these things not happened to me, I would not be who I am today. I developed a tough skin from this and I am positive that without this I would not be as confident and sure of myself as I am today. I find pride in my ability to walk away from certain situations, but I also understand those who can't. Love is a drug in itself and a combination of the two can ultimately lead to destruction until you are forced to look at yourself in the mirror and no longer recognize the person you see. And from that I am a better person.

Have you ever been in a dangerous situation that you were afraid to walk away from? If so, what was it?

___

What kept you there?

___

CONFESSION:

REFLECTION:

> *"Since we cannot change reality, let us change the eyes which see reality."*
> *- Nikos Kazantzakis*

2 THE REALITY CHECK

Not knowing what's going to happen next in life can be scary—especially following a series of events that you were sure would destroy you. When your entire world shifts and everything you knew to be normal doesn't seem as realistic anymore, the reality of having to accept that you have to make adjustments to your new life will settle. Throughout the first year of my son's life I received no contact from his father and although I knew that things would be like this, it wasn't until that first year closed that I officially accepted that I would have to take this journey on solo.

After my son turned one I decided it was time to move out of my parents' house and stop being dependent on the things I needed to grow out of. It was comfortable to be there. I had no bills and could pretty much come and go as I pleased. However, I was twenty-six years old, a mother, and back working full time. I attended class full time during the day and worked from five to eleven in the evenings. Thankfully I had parents willing to take on the responsibility of caring for my son during the evenings while I worked. In my mind this was the perfect time to make a change. The reality was that it was time to suck up my fears and dissatisfaction with my situation and change it.

I went apartment shopping and found a place I could afford, although it was not in an ideal neighborhood. To ease the burden of bills, a friend and I decided to move into the apartment together. The day I signed my lease for my new apartment I was again told I would be laid off from my job. Though this was an unfortunate circumstance, the lease had already been signed and there was no turning back from there. We moved in and within a month, luckily, I was able to find another job. Continually attempting to embrace fear.

Following what I thought could be the beginning of a breakthrough, I was faced with circumstances that seemed to provide a firm slap in the face. I was laid off for the third time, though with more luck I was able to pick up a few part-time jobs that helped me keep up with the bills, but not before I was faced with collection notices and a car repossession. This was a point in my life when I felt rock bottom couldn't get any closer.

I've always heard people say that things will get completely out of control before they will get better, but at that point I didn't see the possibility of things getting any better. I also didn't see how I would possibly be able to find a way out of the hole I was digging myself into, mentally and financially. I blamed myself. I started experiencing the feeling you get when you ask yourself, "What next?" and "Why did I put myself in this situation?"

While all of the craziness was going on I continued to go to class, driving the booger green Oldsmobile that belonged to my grandmother, anticipating graduation. At that point in my life I learned more about myself than I think I ever will. I thought I was above having to drive an ugly car, although it was providing me the very same transportation back and forth to class that my previous car provided. I was ashamed to be seen in the car and always parked as far away as possible from the school so that no one would see me driving it. Ultimately, I thought I was too good for a reality check. The true reality in this situation, that I see now but didn't see then, is that this car, as ugly as it was, was a blessing that I never recognized. It got me back in forth to class for my final semester in college and got me to the stadium on the day of my graduation. It gave me the opportunity to accomplish a goal many didn't think I would. Situations that challenge who you are have their way of revealing what they are really about later.

These experiences gave me a full understanding of what life was truly about: making decisions. For every decision you make you will indeed be faced with the fallout from it. I made the decision to take on motherhood under unfortunate circumstances, I made the decision to move out of my parents' house at a time that I may not have been ready to take it on, and I made the decision to take it all for what it was worth. But the common factor I notice in these things is that I was responsible for each one of them. From this I learned that it's not what life throws at you, it's about how you catch it.

There were times that quitting school and getting a full-time job seemed like a better option. I even had several people suggest that I give up my dream of finishing college and just go back later. But I had people to prove wrong. There were friends and family that never expected to see me graduate and only possessed high hopes for me but accepted that I would never really accomplish the things they hoped I would. There were times during my reality check that I was willing to accept that I would disappoint a few and didn't care. I even felt myself willing to accept less than I should for a quick fix. That's when I realized that the one person I needed to prove wrong was myself. From this, I eventually became pissed off with my situation and even more pissed off with the complacency I felt creeping in. Then I learned that the true reality check in this wasn't that I was struggling as a result of my decisions. The reality was that I was the only person capable of and responsible for making these decisions work. I couldn't let my struggles define me. I had to find a way to let them develop me.

For many people, including myself at the time, the idea of a quick fix is great, until you have to face the reality that things are not completely settled until you actually face the truth and deal with it. When I say deal with it I don't mean simply accepting it for what it's worth, I mean actually handling the situation.

My reality was that I was now a mom, a college graduate, and lost. Part of this reality was that I had to stop looking at myself as defeated. I had to stop replaying the past over and over in my head. I had to stop worrying about the things that could have been. I shifted my focus from the list of things I had to do for my son to a list of things I needed to do for myself to be a better mother for him. The fear I felt had to be replaced with determination. This determination was to become much more than I ever imagined. There comes a point where you have to stop feeling sorry for yourself and thinking people will feel sorry for you because of your circumstances. You have to give yourself a break because things won't be perfect. Just be willing to roll with the punches.

To handle my situation, I had to decide what I wanted out of life. For a person who has always been focused on the "right now" in life, it can be difficult to nail these things down. For me, I found difficultly in recognizing that things will no longer be handed to me. I made the decision to drop my concerns about what other people thought and wanted for me and embrace, for the first time in my life, what I thought and wanted for myself. And I was the person to make these decisions, regardless of what anyone else thought about it.

What experiences have you had that dropped reality on your plate?

___

Are you still experiencing the idea of resting in this situation, or are you moving forward? What can you do to move forward from this?

___

CONFESSION:

REFLECTION:

"People don't suddenly change, you just suddenly see the real them."
- Michelle Blanchard

3 WHAT THEY SAY

As a woman I think it is second nature to receive advice, whether wanted or unwanted, on any given day. Regardless of the topic, as women we tend to think that because we've had similar experiences, we have the right to provide advice to one another. I've always been one of those people—offering advice when it wasn't requested. I have since learned how annoying it can be to receive unsolicited advice.

Since I became a mother I have received an abundance of advice, much of which I smiled and listened through and left the conversation rolling my eyes because in my mind there was no way their advice applied to me. Some of this I look back on and realize that the advice could have been helpful if I was more open to receiving it.

It took me a very long time to understand the concept of not caring what other people thought. Yes, your reputation is everything, but the most important thing to remember is that most of the people that find pleasure in judging and pointing out our failures are usually not the people that genuinely have any true importance in our lives. As free willed as I was, I still wanted to be accepted, wanted to be loved, and I cared a lot about what other people thought. Yet I never let it hinder what I was going to do and what I wasn't.

I've had friends offer me advice and say unfavorable things about me. I've been told that people will never take me seriously as a businessperson because of who I used to be. I've even received unfavorable responses to my goals and have seen the look of disbelief on the faces of these very same people when I've expressed my accomplishments and success. I've also received advice that, had I followed it, would have left me stuck in a place far below what I know I could accomplish. I think some people find difficulty in accepting that a single mom with real life experience can use those same difficult experiences to build a better life.

When people offer advice, it comes from many different places. For some people, they think the advice they give is great and helpful regardless of whether it is or not. And then there are some people that offer advice from a cold, devious, and envious place. This advice can leave you feeling low and sometimes angry if you aren't able to process the place it comes from. Also, keep in mind that a lot of this advice is not given to you. It's for you, but delivered to someone else in the form of "She needs to…" or "I wish she would just…" and "Somebody needs to tell her…."

Negative forms of advice will come from many different directions and there will always be someone with something to say. These are the things that women have to recognize and learn from. Take the advice for what it's worth, but also recognize the place the advice is coming from. Some advice that feels negative can actually be the truth of your situation, wrapped in a bad package.

I have the pleasure of spending a lot of time with all types of women—married, divorced, single, and especially women with children. From these conversations I find myself feeling extremely blessed for my situation while they tend to feel sorry for me, thinking that it must be awful to do it alone—and for some women it is, but for me, my appreciation is in consistency. Stories of husbands not helping out or traveling much of the time with a new job or some divorcees left to learn how to handle it alone after having the support previously makes me grateful for a consistent journey. It has always been just us and I feel lucky that I have not had to experience what many of these women have. When you are faced with difficulties, you will learn to find joy in the most unconventional things. I had no idea when my struggle began that I would later appreciate it. Knowing and learning an appreciation for my circumstances and how easily things could be worse helped me develop an understanding that what someone else thinks is far less important than what I know.

As a single mother and woman, it can feel good to

talk to another woman about her experiences and gain advice on how to handle certain situations. And there will always be a woman willing to give you advice on how to handle things.

One of the most important things that I learned is that every woman's journey is not the same. Once I realized this, I became a lot better off. Just like anything that challenges you in life, motherhood challenged me and brought on some struggles. But it's life and you can't walk around mad at the world over a life only you can live. Some people will not like you and not everyone will find you attractive. But how can these opinions elevate you? Don't let challenges and opinions discourage you.

There can be difficulty in not allowing someone else's opinion and advice get to us, and the hardest part of that can be accepting that you control how these things make you feel. We are in control of our own feelings and we can cut back on how things negatively affect us by not comparing our situation to the next persons. While your struggles may seem greater, that doesn't mean they are. It just means that person may have mastered a way to use their struggles as opportunities.

As I reflect on all the things I received advice on from other women, the one thing I wished I was advised on was my ability to take on any journey that I wanted. I wish I had been told that I could start my own business. I wish I had been encouraged to never take no for an answer. I wish someone told me that no one is going to give me all the things I want, but that I possess the ability to get things for myself. Regardless of what anyone has said or what advice has been given, your journey is yours. Make your greatest struggles work for you.

Have you received advice that hurt, but you later recognized it as being legitimate advice in a bad package? What was it?

_____

_____

_____

_____

_____

_____

_____

_____

_____

_____

Have you ever felt discouraged after talking to someone? How did this make you feel? How can you overcome it?

_____

_____

_____

_____

_____

_____

_____

_____

What ways do/could you encourage the people in your life?

What have been your greatest struggles? How can you make these struggles work for you?

CONFESSION:

REFLECTION:

"Nothing ever becomes real till it is experienced."
- John Keates

4 EXPERIENCE, NOT BAGGAGE

As we go through life, we are all faced with different experiences that tend to stay with us. These experiences can come from relationships, friendships, family issues, the loss of a loved one, and many other things. Each of these things can leave a lasting impression on how we approach the remainder of our lives. People tend to use the word "baggage" when referring to something that we carry with us through our lives. If someone enters a new relationship with reservations from previous relationship, we call that "baggage." If someone is mistreated by their family or friend and present caution about how they approach things the next time, it's classed as "baggage."

We have to stop considering these things baggage because we experience each and every situation for a reason. What you take from it is where the grey area begins. I find it easier to look at these things as an experience, not baggage. For example, when you leave a job that you didn't like, which provided you the opportunity to gain knowledge about the field, you still have the experience. You wouldn't go to the next job with a negative attitude simply because the previous job wasn't a good fit. Normally we leave those situations happy to be moving on to our next venture. We can apply this same model of thinking to other parts of our lives as well. It's not easy but it can be done.

As women, relationships can leave lasting impressions on us and tend to shape how we develop and approach other relationships. The experiences from a relationship may cause some women to be apprehensive about dating because of them. It can also make some women very angry, bitter and broken. These feelings are understood by most, but are also a hindrance to your progression.

Following the situation with my son's father, it could be very easy for me to walk around harboring anger and resentment with the decision he made not to be in his son's life. However, that was HIS decision to make. I watch the women around me go through challenges and changes with the fathers' of their children and it's hurtful to watch a person attempt to FORCE someone to take care of their responsibilities. In these situations, the best thing to do is to start making proactive decisions. Ask yourself some questions. Am I going to put him on child support due to his lack of effort to this situation? Is it worth my peace of mind to force him to do what he doesn't want to do? Who is really winning and losing in this situation? These are all questions I asked myself before I made the decision that none of it was worth my sanity. My decision was to never force an unwanted situation. I always felt my son would eventually be the one who would suffer in the end and if he was going to suffer, it wouldn't be because Mommy is constantly frustrated and going to court because his father wasn't doing what he was supposed to. Nor would it be because I was stressed due to the disappointment of him not showing up again when he was supposed to. Just as easily as he made his decision to get lost, I made mine to let him.

While every relationship and every situation is different, the hurt surrounding them can feel the same. The things that make each situation the same is the fact that, at the end of the day, decisions still have to be made. Your relationship hurt could come from someone walking out on you without an explanation; perhaps being cheated on or a series of lies. Regardless of the reason, the pain behind it can hang around for a while.

The circumstances of situations like these may leave you feeling like you need to have your guard up as you approach your next potential relationship, but that's not necessary if you brought your experience with you. Now you know what to look for, what to avoid and you know the warning signs. This doesn't mean you hold someone else accountable for something you should have dealt with personally before you decided to move on, it just means you have the experience that shows you how to handle yourself.

We don't have the ability to force someone to see

who we are. And no effort to force someone to be with you will work. The person we think we are may not be the person they see and the truth of the matter, as hard as it may be, is that we may also not be what they want. These are things we have to accept, take the experience and make our best efforts to move on. You can make these realizations and decisions and apply them to any relationship.

As women, we allow ourselves to cast friendships off much easier than we will relationships. Friendships are supposed to be the things that bring us both joy and happiness. For most people, friendships are an outlet and can possess the qualities of family, so when issues come up in them, a level of distrust may ensue that prevents us from wanting to form those bonds again. Many of us have experienced disappointment from a friend that left us cautious, but does that mean we should change who we are because this disappointment hurt us? We usually don't. We will allow these bonds to disintegrate very easily, while holding on to the idea of a previous unhealthy relationship that wasn't meant to be, for years.

I've met a lot of people over the years, which has

left me with a better understanding of what I want and what I don't want and the types of people I like to spend my time around. This includes relationships, friendships and family. I've experienced being a mom—the good, the bad, and the ugly. I've experienced being the friend with the best advice when a friend is in a bad situation. And I've also experienced a four-year period of being alone to learn myself.

You are in control of the things that make you happy. I think it's important to understand that you can't expect people to make you happy if you don't genuinely know how to do it for yourself. Carrying around hurt and frustration isn't beneficial to any of us, but having experience is. Experience means you've learned something and now know how to apply it. Life teaches us these things for a reason. So, any struggle you've experienced or are experiencing from a relationship is shaping who you are about to become, but it is not who you are. It's simply providing you with the necessary experience you need to get through.

What efforts have you made to learn what genuinely makes you happy?

_____

_____

_____

_____

_____

_____

_____

_____

_____

_____

Have you had the opportunity to take time to yourself and focus on you? If not, what keeps you from doing this?

_____

_____

_____

_____

_____

_____

_____

_____

Where do you find your happiness?

_____

_____

_____

_____

_____

_____

_____

_____

_____

_____

CONFESSION:

REFLECTION:

"No matter how many times people try to criticize you, the best revenge is to prove them wrong."
- Zayn Malik

5 PROVE THEM WRONG

When I first decided to start my own business, I didn't receive a lot of positive support—not even from the places I expected to receive it most. Family, friends, and strangers tend to misunderstand your goals simply because they can't see themselves doing it. Dreaming to do something outside of the ordinary is often met with misunderstanding and unacceptance and can be attributed to the fact that the person you are expressing these things to is uncomfortable with accepting the fact that you dream bigger than they do. I don't care what your goal is—you can accomplish it with the right amount of work.

Ten years ago there was no way someone could have told me that one day someone would say to me "I look up to you" or "You inspire me." Nor could anyone have told me that I would have my own business that is thriving and growing more and more each day. If your goal is to go to law school, do that. If the goal is to be a business owner, be that. If your goal is to be an actress, be that. Just give it all you have. Don't allow any opinion or comment be the reason you don't chase and accomplish your dream. If I'd have listened to every sideways acknowledgement about my dream to start and successfully run my own business I would still be in the very same miserable places as those who gave it to me are. It's not hard to recognize when someone is genuinely happy for you. Choose friends carefully and don't be afraid to lose a few along the way.

I've lost a few friends along the way—never burning bridges, but also understanding that not everyone will be on board and sometimes they need to be left behind. Old friends will have a hard time seeing you evolve into someone better than what they may want you to be. Good friends will evolve with you. Women have a hard time competing in so many aspects that the last place we should feel the need to compete is against one another. Becoming a mother opened my eyes to this, as I watch my son grow and I recognize that he will soon start developing lifelong friendships that may disappoint him. How do I advise him on the importance of choosing the people you allow in your life carefully and not being afraid to drop a few?

As women, we have a responsibility for each other. We are often seen as weak and single mothers are often characterized as a source that produces less productive and accomplished children. The only way to change this is by changing your way of thinking to prove them wrong.

I was once one of those women who laughed and snickered about other women and even mothers that seemed to be struggling, thinking I was much better off than they were. I wasn't mature enough to realize that while I laughed, the source that brought humor to me was a part of me that was just as miserable as I thought they were.

Becoming a mother changed just about every aspect of thinking for me. I feel an immediate closeness to all women as I try to relate to them regardless of the attitudes and action they display toward me. I realize the issue is much deeper than their exterior. We are all beaten down in some aspect of our lives. To think otherwise is to not accept that there are things about us that aren't perfect. Children think purely, not judging but instead accepting you for who you are and looking in excitement at the things we say we will do. I would never tell my son he can't be something or can't do something. We grow up being told we can be anything we want to be. Where did that change? I was reminded of the purity of a child's thinking the day I told my son I was going to write a book. His first response was "You can do it, Mommy. Are you gonna write about me?" He followed that up with, "After you write your book a lot of people will probably want to read it." Not one thought came into his mind that he should attempt to deter me from doing something I wanted. He not only immediately believed in me, but he also embodied the capability to look at it on a much bigger scale than I did.

My goal is to consistently prove every person who has an opinion about me wrong—except, of course, the people who genuinely support me. My goal with them is to exceed the expectations they had for my success. If setting small goals is easier, do that. Me, I set my goals extremely high—that way, when I reach them, I surprise even myself. There isn't enough time to sit back and wait for things to shake on their own. I refuse to sit back and allow my child to see me fall into the expectations of small-minded individuals and have him think anything less than that his mother changed her life to build a much better one for him.

As adults, we can learn from children in the way that we think and treat each other. We have to stop the idea of trying to discourage someone from doing something they want to do and we have to stop allowing people to discourage us from the things we want to do. You do this by only feeling the desire to impress yourself. If you find the ability to impress yourself, your worst critic, then you will certainly find your ability to prove any and everyone else wrong.

The difficulty I find in proving people wrong is that some people will still find it hard to accept things, even after you have achieved your goal. We all know that person—the one that will find the negativity in every situation and grab at any attempt to make you feel less than they are. I like to call them "what if" and "I heard" people. They tend to think they are providing constructive feedback, but you know what it's really about. For example, you just made the decision to step out, try a new venture, and you decide to tell your friends and family. The conversation will go a little something like this:

You: "I've been meaning to tell you that I decided to start selling cosmetics on the side for some extra income."

The "I heard" person: "I heard you have to buy the product before you can start selling it."

The "what if" person: "What if it doesn't work and you waste your money?"

While these people feel they are asking valid questions (and they very well may be), in these questions I find the doubt in their minds that I have the capability of forming and taking all of these questions into consideration without them having to mention it. We all understand that friends are supposed to challenge you and give you honest feedback, but we also need to understand that sometimes support is all that's needed.

I learned the hard way about these types of people and often allowed their feedback to deter me from the things I wanted to do. Once I matured enough to understand how to handle these situations I learned that the best thing to do is to pick and choose the things you share until you have already successfully started working on the venture. It may not be easy and it's very possible that they will catch wind of it and be upset that they weren't informed previously. From this you will get a "You didn't have to tell me" or "When were you going to tell me" phone call—and that's okay.

We have to learn that the important things don't require any stamps of approval from the people who doubt you. It's more important to see the saltiness they feel after you exceed all of the things they thought you couldn't. It's also more important that your initial goal in accomplishing these things is that it is for you and secretly, to prove them wrong. Many of them will never admit that you are great, even after the evidence is on the table; however, the feeling you get within yourself after you recognize your progress is always the most important factor.

Have you ever felt like you couldn't live up to the expectations someone had for you, or that no matter what you did you wouldn't be good enough? How did that make you feel?

___

___

___

___

___

___

___

___

What have you done to make yourself proud?

___

___

___

___

___

___

___

___

CONFESSION:

REFLECTION:

"Every job is good if you do your best work and work hard. A man who works hard stinks only to those that have nothing to do but smell."
- Laura Ingalls Wilder

6 BE YOUR BEST YOU

As individuals, we all have very different lives to live. We can't live our lives trying to please others while forgetting about taking care of the things that make you happy. For many years I lived trying to convince others that I was good enough. Truthfully, you will never be good enough for some and you will never be able to live up to the standards that others have set for you.

Your parents may have always pushed you to become a doctor or lawyer without realizing that you have no desire to become either of those. And for some of us, the idea of doing what others want us to do could eventually drive us down the road of unhappiness.

Learning who you are and what you were called here to do is going to be the key to what makes you successful. When (and only when) you are able to determine these things, will you be able to ultimately put yourself in a position to thrive in a way that will make you happy. There may be things that you thrive in along the road, but they may not be the things that make you happy. The past seven or eight years have been nothing short of a struggle for me—and I don't mean physically or financially, I mean mentally. I've struggled with finding myself, finding the things that make me happy and figuring out the things that don't, figuring out what I'm good at and finding a way to channel all of that into becoming a person that is aware.

Through this, you learn how to love yourself through situations and that isn't easy. I believe that within every situation and circumstance is a lesson. Sometimes the lesson strengthens you and sometimes it breaks you, and losing yet another job last year gave me the perfect opportunity to break. Instead, I looked at it as a time to reflect and figure out exactly what my next step would be. My bumpy ride taught me that no situation is worth losing my mind over. Instead, I love myself through the situation. By this I mean I allow myself to feel the situation while reminding myself of what is most important.

We will never be exactly what everyone else wants us to be. We can only be the best person that we can be for ourselves. I'm satisfied with being a single mother, doing what I love, and understanding that I may always be the sole provider for my household. I didn't always feel this way. There were times that I felt I would only be happy if I had someone else there to take it on with me. In that feeling, I felt incomplete and incapable of doing the things I wanted because I thought I needed someone else there. It wasn't until I realized that I was good enough to do it on my own and love myself that I realized I then possessed the ability to eventually allow someone else in.

Through this I developed the ability to understand the position my son Reece's dad may have been in and I forgive him for disappearing. There will be days I am frustrated and then I remember there have been responsibilities that I have run away from before as well. Regardless of the size of the responsibility, fear is what leads us away from them.

Today, I live for Reece and myself. I strive to only impress him and me, but find it interesting to prove a few wrong along the way. Worrying about what others think and want from you will only leave you exhausted. Think of who you admire most. Now count on one hand the people who are not impressed with them. It's likely not possible. Everyone has critics. It's how you process them that is important. Allow them to criticize, but don't give them the ammo to support their criticisms. My greatest struggle provided my best opportunity because it gave me something and someone else to live for.

There are people that think some people are luckier than others. I disagree. I will not credit anything I've accomplished or overcome to luck. I simply uncovered my dreams, let go of the things that held me back, and found something else to focus on. After doing that, I worked for it. So while it may seem like someone has luck on his or her side, consider what struggles may have gone on behind the scenes that led them to that point.

Being your best you means that you do your best to satisfy the things within you that push you. What things make you happy? If you can answer that question then you know what you need to focus on. If you aren't able to answer that question then the first place you can find those things is within yourself. If you only find your happiness in someone else then your main focus should be on discovering ways that you can make yourself happy if they weren't there.

Take the things that you are good at and mold them into something you can be proud of. Be someone that you can be proud of. I once found it difficult to look in the mirror and say "You're awesome." It sounds weird, but it's something I had to learn to do because I had to learn to become my best cheerleader. Continue to strive for better in your friendships, relationships, careers, motherhood, etc., while remembering that the only person who is going to make it happen for you is you. Be your best! But more importantly, be your best you!

What are your dreams?

_____

_____

_____

_____

_____

_____

_____

_____

_____

_____

Are you working towards accomplishing them? If not, what is stopping you? If so, what progress have you seen?

_____

_____

_____

_____

_____

_____

_____

_____

_____

CONFESSION:

REFLECTION:

ABOUT THE AUTHOR

Erika Dawkins is a freelance writer, an editor, the owner of It's Only Write Communications, and most importantly, a mom. Erika has a Bachelor's in Print Communications and a Master's in Media Communications and has spend the past 11 years writing and contributing for several print and online publications. She currently works with businesses and individuals in finding their voices through effective communications. Erika recently set her writing focus on encouraging and motivating other women to pursue their dreams. For more information about the author please visit:
www.erikadawkins.com

Made in the USA
Charleston, SC
13 February 2015